Harvest Festival

Nancy Dickmann

www.raintreepublishers.co.uk
Visit our website to find out
more information about
Raintree books.

To order:
☎ Phone 0845 6044371
▤ Fax +44 (0) 1865 312263
✉ Email myorders@raintreepublishers.co.uk

Customers from outside the UK please telephone +44 1865 312262

Raintree is an imprint of Capstone Global Library Limited, a company incorporated in England and Wales having its registered office at 7 Pilgrim Street, London, EC4V 6LB – Registered company number: 6695582

Text © Capstone Global Library Limited 2011
First published in hardback in 2011
First published in paperback in 2012
The moral rights of the proprietor have been asserted.

Edited by Sian Smith, Nancy Dickmann, and Rebecca Rissman
Designed by Steve Mead
Picture research by Elizabeth Alexander
Production by Victoria Fitzgerald
Originated by Capstone Global Library Ltd
Printed and bound in China by South China Printing Company Ltd

ISBN 978 0 431 00731 1 (hardback)
14 13 12 11 10
10 9 8 7 6 5 4 3 2 1

ISBN 978 1 406 21930 2 (paperback)
15 14 13 12 11
10 9 8 7 6 5 4 3 2 1

British Library Cataloguing in Publication Data
Dickmann, Nancy.
  Harvest festival. -- (Holidays and festivals)
  1. Harvest festivals--Pictorial works--Juvenile
  literature.
  I. Title II. Series
  394.2'64-dc22

Acknowledgements
We would like to thank the following for permission to reproduce photographs: © Capstone Global Library Ltd p. **15** (Steve Mead); Alamy pp. **9** (© Art Directors & TRIP), **19** (© Alex Segre), **20** (© Image Source); Getty Images pp. **12**, **23 top middle** (Pieter the Younger Brueghel/The Bridgeman Art Library), **13** (Hulton Archive); iStockphoto p. **22 top right** (© Paul Cowan); Photolibrary pp. **8**, **23 top** (Howard Sokol/Index Stock Imagery), **14** (Roger Cope/Britain on View), **16** (Clare Roberts/The Travel Library), **18**, **22 bottom right** (Andrew Sydenham/Fresh Food Images), **21** (Brand X Pictures); Shutterstock pp. **5** (© Andrejs Pidjass), **6**, **23 bottom** (© Elena Elisseeva), **7**, **23 bottom middle** (© Jose Ignacio Soto), **11**, **22 bottom left** (© Viktor1), **22 top left** (© Tereza Dvorak); The Bridgeman Art Library p. **10** (Lhermitte, Leon Augustin /Musee des Beaux-Arts/Lauros/Giraudon); World Religions Photo Library pp. **4**, **17**.

Front cover photograph of wheatsheaf loaf and harvest festival produce reproduced with permission of Photolibrary (Andrew Sydenham/Fresh Food Images). Back cover photograph reproduced with permission of Shutterstock (© Andrejs Pidjass).

We would like to thank Diana Bentley, Dee Reid, Nancy Harris, and Richard Aubrey for their invaluable help in the preparation of this book.

Every effort has been made to contact copyright holders of material reproduced in this book. Any omissions will be rectified in subsequent printings if notice is given to the publishers.

Contents

What is a festival?

A festival is a time when people come together to celebrate.

Harvest festivals happen in the autumn.

Why are harvests celebrated?

crop

Crops are plants that we eat.

wheat

Harvest is the time when crops are
ready to pick.

If the harvest is good, there is enough food to eat.

At a harvest festival people give thanks
for a good harvest.

Harvest festivals long ago

Long ago, the start of the harvest was called Lammas Day.

Lammas loaf

People made special bread from the first crops.

When the harvest was finished, there was a great feast.

People sang and danced to celebrate.

corn dollies

The last corn to be cut was made into corn dollies.

corn dolly

The dollies were put in the fields in the spring.

Harvest festivals today

church

Many churches celebrate harvest festivals.

People bring food to decorate
the church.

bread

Some people bring bread that looks like wheat.

People sing songs and say prayers.

People give thanks for having enough food.

People give food to others who need it.

Things to look for

corn dolly

display of food

Lammas loaf

wheatsheaf loaf

Have you seen these things? They make people think of harvest festivals.

Picture glossary

 **crops** plants that are grown for us to eat

 **feast** big meal for everyone to share

 **harvest** the time when crops are ready to pick. Harvest can also mean the food that is picked.

 **wheat** plant that can be made into flour for baking

Index

Notes for parents and teachers

Before reading

Ask the children to name some of their favourite foods. Discuss where the foods come from. Do some of them grow on farms? Make a list together. Ask the children how they think these foods get from farms to their homes. Do they know when crops are harvested?

After reading

• Teach the children a typical harvest song or hymn, such as *Come, Ye Thankful People, Come* or *First the Seed and Then the Rain*.

• Help the children to decorate harvest hampers. Encourage them to think of symbols or decorations that would be appropriate for an autumn harvest. Talk about how some people may not always have enough to eat. Fill the hampers and donate them to a local food bank or charity.

• Talk about other types of harvest festivals, for example the harvest of the seas, American Thanksgiving celebrations, or the Jewish festival of Sukkot. Explain that many different cultures celebrate harvests. Ask the children why they think that harvests are celebrated in so many different cultures around the world.

24